WITHOUT CEREMONY

Angela Carr
Without Ceremony

Book*hug Press
Toronto

Library and Archives Canada Cataloguing in Publication

Title: Without ceremony / Angela Carr.
Names: Carr, Angela, 1976– author.
Description: Poems.
Identifiers: Canadiana (print) 20200306715 | Canadiana (ebook) 2020030674x
    ISBN 9781771666299 (softcover) | ISBN 9781771666305 (EPUB)
    ISBN 9781771666312 | ISBN 9781771666329 (Kindle)
Classification: LCC PS8605.A7728 W58 2020 | DDC C811/.6—dc23

Printed in Canada

The production of this book was made possible through the generous
assistance of the Canada Council for the Arts and the Ontario Arts Council.
Book*hug Press also acknowledges the support of the Government of Canada
through the Canada Book Fund and the Government of Ontario through the
Ontario Book Publishing Tax Credit and the Ontario Book Fund.

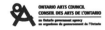

Book*hug Press acknowledges that the land on which we operate is the
traditional territory of many nations, including the Mississaugas of the
Credit, the Anishnabeg, the Chippawa, the Haudenosaunee and the Wendat
peoples. We recognize the enduring presence of many diverse First Nations,
Inuit, and Métis peoples and are grateful for the opportunity to meet and
work on this territory.

Contents

1   Direction of Flight

9   Iceberg Blue

16   Practice before Theory

17   Straight as an Arrow

18   Around/Harmonically Static

19   Angels

21   Catalogue of Disasters

23   The Music Did Demand Certain Things

25   Proving Up for Honey

26   Marginalia

27   Going through the Motions

28   Blue Arrows

29   Without Ceremony

30   A Morbid Occupation

31   Feminine Rhyme

32   Reusable Swerve

33   An Opening

34   Falling Arrows

36   Enter on the Left

37   Strange but True

38   A Held Note

39 The Sculptor's House

40 Eva Hesse's Arrows

41 St. Augustine's Arrow

42 Palm Reading, after Joan
   Mitchell's *No Rain*

43 Island of Broken Arrows,
   Incandescent, Transient

44 Moving Platform

46 Plot Line, after "The Green
   Years" (*Os Verdes Anos*)

47 Relocation

49 Colour Debts

50 Demolition

51 Genitalia

53 Requiem

65 Quiver

67 Hardwick

77 Briefing

79 I was quite still for a long time

87 *Notes on the poems*

Direction of Flight

[1]

At the fish market in Union Square we choose flounder filleted
and decline the oysters.

From an elderly farmer who looks like your grandfather,
we buy six narcissi: his only product.

They're a pale buttery yellow, flecked with old-fashioned Monarch orange,
a colour scheme from your grandmother's breakfast nook, a scene that vanished in the twentieth

century, as quickly as this perfume is subtle, yet the aroma does not know how to fill the subway car.
A man hovering over us near the doors asks what they are, says he only knows roses.

He nudges awake a passenger seated on the short bench made for one, tells him, make some space,
and takes a seat on the edge. When we pass him, exiting the subway, he bids us

goodbye in a whisper. Next time he will look for narcissi,
heedless suns that push through crowds, always ahead of time.

[2]

Midway through dinner a rash erupts across my face and shoulders.
Pomegranate-red raised hives: I'm flushed with toxins.

I sleep furtively, blinds lightly smacking the windowsill in the wind.
Heraclitus says all things are in flux and there is no unity

but in flux. In America, we plummet or flourish.
In the news this morning, the only story I read is the unexplained

death of Justice Sheila Abdus-Salaam, whose body was found floating
in the Hudson at 1:45 a.m. at West 132nd Street, West Harlem. She

wrote a judgment establishing non-biological parents' rights. You call to me
from the living room, also reading this story. The poem is supposed to float

between us, but mine goes under the moment the language of the law is introduced.
I am still florid this morning, weak with the bruised language of allergies.

[3]

To write such a judgment must require equal measures of deliberateness and delicacy.
She is not the *other mother*, the *inferior mother*, the *mother-helper*,

as she often gripes. She is grateful to the judge she has never known,
alive in the springtime of a law that knows her reality.

There is more light reflecting off of every surface. I scrutinize the awkward
prepositions "off of" and decide to keep them, grain in the film. On the way to see *Wanda*

at the Metrograph Rep Cinema, we're on the F train and two men
seated on opposite sides of the car are conversing. Standing between them, I feel compelled

to move aside so they can see each other speak. "Did you see the story about the judge?"
"Fucked-up shit, man. I only saw the headline." "Do they have a suspect?" "Not yet."

I am silent. It's nearly Easter. I lack reverence for tradition, but the subway car
is holy. By nightfall, the police will have decided the judge committed suicide

because her mother and brother committed suicide on Easter, a painful anniversary.
No one is satisfied with this explanation.

[4]

Barbara Loden's *Wanda* was inspired by a headline about a robbery accomplice:
Woman Thanks Judge Who Sentences Her to Prison. Who is this woman who says thanks?

She's a drifter from a mining town who has an empty purse. She barely flinches when he slaps her.
She's hungry and numb, poverty without end, dependent, desperate. She's also beautiful

but abject and therefore dismissed as stupid, because she's beautiful and abject.
She struggles to read the newspaper, slow and uncertain. She's homeless

like Agnes Varda's vagabond or Tess of the d'Ubervilles, fictional heroines.
But Barbara Loden *is* Wanda and her scenes are mostly improvised. She's also the director wearing

the pants her partner tries to throw out the window. All this symmetry makes me weep: she
plays the powerless onscreen but is omnipotent behind the scene. I weep

for the absence of tears *when the flower opens and reveals the heart it does not have.*
The tragedy of *Wanda* is lack, that hope is withheld absolutely, that she remains forever ignorant

of what she should want. All she knows is what she has rejected and she arrives at nothing.

[5]

There will be more for her to reject, but so much time wasted in the process. Daffodil petals
are frail in your hands, yet the flowers regain their strength in a vase with water. The law

of water is that its colour will change. Icarus flies into the sun. Adolescent, he desires the highs
of lawless experience. Wings melted, wax mixing with pond water, he floats on his back. His father

built sturdy wings and imparted his knowledge. Then, like a couplet,
they burst into impossible flight together. This structure was not to last.

The law of flight is contained in the heart of the daffodil. The law of revolution
is renewed in the heart of flight. The law of knowledge is carried by Icarus

where it changes too quickly to name.

[6]

In *Landscape Crossed by a River, with the Fall of Icarus*, faint whitecaps on the water
could be feathers from wasted wings. The boy's flailing limbs, although disproportionately

large, are ignored by the onlookers. A seamless horizon exchanges values
of sea and sky, uninterrupted and impassive. To everyone else, Icarus is an afterthought.

Even in Bruegel's title, he's an afterthought. Nudged into memory by the flickering cursor.
Spring wants to pour onto us the warmth of forgetting despite the small flags that tighten within us.

Scars at the tips of ship masts are icons, curling sails are ribbons in the importunate
hair of girlhood. Your heart bends forward toward nightfall.

You will never know whether their impassivity is ignorance. You need to press
your face into the daffodils to smell their perfume. You need to leap from your easy

passivity and be prepared to swim. An index finger is missing
from a statue on the pier. It must have pointed outward, but to what?

A child looks in the direction of her mother's missing finger. Its absence is only secondary
to the absence of what it pointed to. To the mother's knowledge

all else is parenthetical.

[7]

Poem crossed by an avenue with the fall of daffodils.
Two rivers with the fall of roses,
with the fall of night, with the fall of our lovers, who were persuaded,
with wax that melts, with film that decays, without direction, inside an absence, under layers of law,
imposing upon them, with the fall of peoples, with the fall of curtains, with the fall of paper,
with persistence, without distinction, if that within them, if that is in them/

April 12–15, 2017

Iceberg Blue

[1]

Searching for a volume of Pope's *Homer*
that concludes with an index of similes,
I reach into the solitary spaces between shelves
built like utilitarian couplets,
hidden structures of memory.
A broken exit sign hangs at an awkward
angle from the ceiling,
vaguely glowing and adrift over dark stacks.

When the library's antique elevator opens,
its retracting gate
releases ominously. It's an apostrophe
to the reader whose hands hold
the words of more ghosts,
            other haunted idioms.

This is confessional:
I read because
I forget easily
            and I want to taste
all the stars in a clear night sky.

I ask Lucretius what he would have written
about light pollution. The smallest mote
of illumination, finest powder in the inhaler.
We are also of paper, of ink, of corticosteroids, of dust,
of the parenthetical lung,
of green tea, gravel, and gorsebushes
born onto the "shores of light"
(also translated as "borders of light").

[2]

I read because
the neutral
measure of prose
becomes ferocious
in the dolorous mouth
whose words
are sovereign
grief.

Because
to remember
the oblong *o*
of a necklace pendant
is to intercept
geometry's first
space and line.

I read because of air and brume,
cloud cover and deluge, of the delay
that is buoyancy, of cocks
and coaches, of menagerie:
because of alphabets and beasts,
        because the alphabet is a certain
beast that coalesces only
in the overcast
drift and I desire
breath and air
and I desire
its intension.

[3]

Lucretius takes the elevator to the fifth floor, key for room five in his hand.
Alone in the elevator, he regards his reflection fearlessly, critically:
his ruddy skin, windblown grey hair,
in the full-length mirror. His ample form,
shadows of Latin, translations
of doubt. He wonders whether he should lock
the door to his study room. He recalls
a camouflage military knapsack
on the floor of the subway, deposited close to a door.
Also the sealed train walls, Bombardier-made,
seamlessly metallic, stretching to infinity.
He recalls a fear of gunfire,
dread of confining developments
and of the traditional narrative arc.

To an impudent and impure girl
in her early twenties he once advised:
your poem must follow an emotional arc.

She was dressed in discarded garments.
The hem of her ankle-length
camel-hair coat was stained with slush and mud.

Her response to the Poet was delayed,
saved for twenty years later.

Lucretius unfolded her note.
What I have felt, she wrote,
has been imperfectly written
yet what I have written
has been perfectly felt.

[4]

Ice absorbs more light from the red
end of the spectrum
and without air
it appears even more blue.

Lucretius projects a picture of the iceberg for his students.

Its frozen form is an absurd source of joy
delivered by currents
and permanently displaced
off the coast of Newfoundland
where it causes tourist traffic jams.

Spring will soon break
across decades of memory-
veined ice.

[5]

In middle age, Lucretius finds he's less flexible,
like a book that, after being
soaked, has dried, pages
warped and sticking tightly together,
stiff and slow to open.

His intended course is to return to the beginning again.

He will wear ice-blue feathers in his wings.
He will outstay attraction, adrift
on a dream of completion.

[6]

Lucretius puts the key to room five in an outer pocket of his black leather shoulder bag.
He dislikes clutter on his desk.
He is composing his last blog post, but it never ends.
Lucretius remains the same: part of a whole, an amount consumed.
At forty-five, Lucretius started to wear
contact lenses because he believed glasses
would obscure his libidinous virility.
He would deny he is lonely, but
his orbit of reference still returns us to room five
where he sits alone.
Lucretius started to write this post when he was a prisoner
of conscience, when the evening star lasted
a very long time, telling
lies about the achievements of every proverb.

Practice before Theory

But one night the door will open and we'll lean into the empty
room where footprints in the dust are impermanent
and prosaic. Idle ink stains on the walls,
a stack of Juicy Fruit on a bookshelf,
shiny balled wrappers, all signs in a mercurial
syntax that evaporates on exposure.
When we are seen as lesbian
they're uncertain which letters have fallen from the tree
and which are bruised, what makes the end of a given word feminine.
The words come to touch us deeply but we keep
them at a distance, sentimental and burning.
A lemon is squeezed
in a country they will never visit
and only fleetingly exists. As you know,
the book does not begin in the liquid state;
just like civility, taste is strongest
when two grounds are opposing
and streams roar, fervent.

Straight as an Arrow

If I begin to write and cross out words
that desire to take flight
and every phrasal verb
that equates civil service with poetry

at the base of the corkwood
an egg's fragmented shell
our last minor birth
retrained by the poem

Around/Harmonically Static

Red is the deepest part of the petal's
fast current, funnels to
flower stamen,
a word of caution
arranged on the other side.
In the Guggenheim,
sunlight's residual
secrecy coils,
a sleeping serpent.
A die-cast friendship
statuette displayed
at home, explicitly
for our reverence.
Nouns devoted to fasting
object strongly
to seed

*by proxy

uprooted.

Angels

I have yet to ask which of the two men in the food truck
is the eponymous Angel: the young man
who pours coffee and changes cash
or the one who cooks eggs rapidly and with flourish,
tossing foil-wrapped sandwiches over his shoulder to be bagged.
And I've never had a conversation with Angelina
who I see even before breakfast
at the gym. All I know about her
is that she's trying to get into shape.
An ampersand of proximity:
we share this name root, *angelus*, ridiculous
for its ethereal purity. Like me, wholly
ordinary, they also, likely,
lack halo and wings. Though one cannot be sure.
We are all immigrants,
which suggests we share
some proficiency in flight.

Then there's Angel Lopez,
who officiates at the Manhattan Marriage Bureau,
every day and first thing in the morning,
ceremoniously without ceremony.
In daily clothes
worn as wedding dress,
newlyweds can travel by subway
directly from there to work.

My high school chemistry teacher was the only
person ever to address me by the diminutive *Angie*.
I won the "Chemistry Award for a Girl"
upon graduation
and did not return for the ceremony.

In any cavity wall
there's a dangerous void, the kind
you shouldn't kid about. Take care
to avoid mistakes;
underground grids
should conduct relatively clean
water throughout the city.

Catalogue of Disasters

I was named after the divine messenger, *Angelus domini*.

They motioned to flick the air above my head and heard a hollow pinging sound
as their fingers struck my invisible halo.

I was raised in the heart of dissatisfaction.
Over the windows hung floor-to-ceiling-length gauzy curtains

in some lights cream-coloured, in others appearing swampy greenish-yellow,
in part because they reflected a moss-coloured carpet, in part

because they were darkened with smoke stains. Smoking and wall-to-wall carpeting
were co-extensive with the suburb where I was raised in the eighties and my childhood.

My first bathing suit was a leopard-print bikini. I read Lucy Maud Montgomery novels by the pool,
at times burning my skin irreparably, squinting at glaring white pages.

I had freckles nearly everywhere and never learned how to twirl a baton.
Early on, I stopped wearing patterned fabrics.

There was a tapestry featuring an owl, as always, above the stairs,
perched in imaginary, shadowy rafters.

We all know descent is most challenging.

They secured clothes on the line with large, pastel-coloured plastic pegs. Folded
cotton fabrics stiffened in the sun. A photographic image, kept in place.

Once, a nude was visible through their compass window
even with the curtains closed.

The suburbs commanded introverts to burn the fossil fuel of their creativity
to make them unable to separate from their context.

Their low, angular slopes sheltered everyone. As though cornered, they were coerced to stay.
The suburbs were the anguish of muted green under the wings of animus.

They refracted rural serenity through a dialogical opposition of toxic fungus
and fungicide, wild pest and pesticide, abjuring privacy.

The Music Did Demand Certain Things

Stubbornly on repeat, a cassette
was stuck in my Ford Granada's ancient tape player
all summer like a settled
idea. In the end
on a late August day
I pulled and the magnetic tape unwound
like fishing line
coming out wet and
blind to its original structure.

A nest of greyish
wrinkled ribbons, later
abandoned by fledglings:
dear suburban memory,
locate the front door
of teenage captivity,
passages swollen/pollen
swallowed in mediocre
pleasures.

On the desk beside *The Politics of Friendship*,
to love magic of proximity
and the past participle
of *to lose*.

It's not a lost cause, to recall
and earmark a memory
for a particular purpose.
Of course, it is dependent on us
but we do not want to impose
our will in spite of it or take
responsibility for its glow
caused by sunlight reflected
or its material demise. The memory
was designed to excavate a compound
long dismissed as impossibly
bodily, a choreography of false starts.

Proving Up for Honey

Honey-coloured frame around a portrait of Lucretius's translator
subdued in honeyed weekend light filtered through dusty blinds.
She regrets her words in an argument about gender and false beginnings,
stylishly holding out against repair.
It's time to revise her argument on knowledge as possession
so she scrutinizes her notes, running out of time, always,
feverish (which sounds just like the Portuguese verb for *to boil*).
Recall, Lucretius, we were once more liquid than this, like honey.
A group of teenage girls barges into the room, bringing delighted
excited energy.
It's contagious.
I wear a butter-coloured
shirt with *Honey* inscribed across my chest
in metallic copper thread.

Marginalia

As though it happened all at once
so the eye could take it in,
medieval illuminated letters shed their illustrations,
which were pushed to the edges of pages
and became marginalia.
Now there is only one ornate letter, the selfie.
I've returned home to intervene in the disaster of my reflection.
No one knows how many intentions are in reserve,
how, by a hairpin, an unexpected phrase
uncovers a patch of wild strawberries
and other minute, trembling memories
stashed under wide lacework
imperceptibly
where the edge becomes the centre,
vanishing in a line of knees on the pavement.

Going through the Motions

Tendons come unstuck.
Poem titles float downriver or are already
within reach. Some have been plucked,
masticated, swallowed. The best
are in our pockets.
Discrete but perfect, they do not let us down.
Don't spend all your titles at once.
I mispell *park* the French way,
disobliged the tremendous finality of *k*.
There are traces of sweetness in this aroma
though it is nearly depleted.
The modesty of *c. Avenue du parc* is so ordinary.
We were practical and purposeful.
We bought lunch in a deli and sat on a bench,
even sunshine a spectacular sight.

Blue Arrows

She cannot say no if the consequence
would be to remove a brick from the building in view of both
but housing neither. They make no effort to change.
It was a friendship of convenience and
repetition. Lights flashing at an intersection
are meant to slow traffic, not halt it altogether.
She knows such deep reverence for the moment when truly
nothing is happening. All dollars are spent to stop time
in this way. I'm pretty sure
the p of inspection invites doodles and marginalia.
We spread an army surplus blanket against the skyline.
She cannot distinguish what type of machinery shimmers
and groans in the near moonlight where
the future is submerged in pounding tides.
Speaking of bridges:
these will also survive us.

Without Ceremony

We entertain impossible postscripts,
substitute "fool" for "malfeasance,"
make friends with fire.
Ah, summer: the firmament sighs.
Cicadas land on eventual dualisms, drowsy.
Language is a drug that keeps us asleep
and awake. With drumsticks,
mulberry, much love:
as though they heard these sounds
for the first time.
Who has been a houseboy?
I am late for the curfew at the hostel, I'll ring
at the beginning again. Now everything
is tarnished and lovely.

A Morbid Occupation

Each word is the shadow of a traffic light
that takes too long to change,
buzzes and blurs under the magnetic red glow
with other shadows cast by innumerable bodies in motion:
agitated bodies with only a docile signal
to stall us in time. At this intersection, drowned by sounds of
tender car horns and abrasive walkie-talkie chatter
drawn under by waves of early, sweet welcome,
among the teeming words, I designed first one eye
then another, as if there could be more than two.
Two, then, we know the personal discomforts
always prominent in the palimpsest but the first to be rubbed out.
Best, I think, to move on, go
on your nerve, turn to the underground nerves
of root vegetables and iris, damp dimensions,
nervous threads of dill, fillets for dinner, oh there we are again *les filles*, girls
and threads, a nervous girl with thread, almost apologizing,
starving her words until they can push
through the eye of a needle.
Did she tell you how real
her fury is, torn always
between the weight of history
or the buoyancy of joy,
surviving to inscribe divergent epistemologies
in stones that do not get buried?

Feminine Rhyme

Every mixture of pen and word partially defeats us.
The poem rattles the spice rack of representation,
striking glass bottles of cached ideas
against one another the way a storm might,
wind embattling the windowpane.
Tonight, the most bitter winter wind:
mere resonance cancels out the perennials' ability to bloom.
I have to see them all at once to acknowledge even one
as though it were a dream that mattered and the garden
emanating from an opening in the wall like a river's embouchure
in the amorphous zone between river and sea,
between poem and cinnamon
scents of roses and lights:
a perfume of stellar complexity.
I still want the humour of your best wishes combined
with *la pensée* of another life
and another language left behind,
melancholic not like a pendulum but a saving
sky that intensifies the totality of our experience
with its warmth
while leaving part of us behind.
In this brief interval I can almost feel
the poem's slight oblivion
though generally its ullage and its umbrage
are imperceptible.

Reusable Swerve

In another version, there are the raw points
I seek for protection
in the northernmost parts of the world
against isolation and fear,
points from which light and heat radiate.
I have a justification for this rationing of words
that received,
reassembled, and deserted us.
They kept them and stocked them up
as they needed,
to survive in the receding occupation
of making do.

An Opening

I suppose the opening protects us from
insularity or short-sightedness
(only in the figurative sense: the retina is already affected),
but what it permits infringes on the perennial fire
of dreams, majestic petals
of the present. Getting a positive result
ten times over, you touch the window gingerly,
caught otherwise in suspense on the opposite side.
I cannot wish you better than I already do, perhaps this is
a serious flaw. My feelings cannot be mere clots
of words in time, addressed to you
and reaching no one.
I wish I could hand you a meaningful, tidy sentence
that would sum it all up,
a cloud of knowledge condensed and shining
in the sudden dawn,
but the letters are nerve endings,
words exposed and wincing.

Falling Arrows

Snow falls in points, not flakes,
raw points that tenderly dive and sway
or pitch forward
into their accumulation as drifts
or oblivion where they melt against the skin.
We should have been experts in the field of snow
but were totally disinterested in its
pithy, unremarkable appearance
as it bore down on us.
This is how I know it is pointed
or rather, that it constitutes "points" in time and space
and thereby invokes a directional force.
These words are stored in a large, earthenware jar
borrowed from antiquity,
a dark winter night with its hard, clear stars
constellate and preserved in place.
The poem has the consistency of frost,
somewhat transparent, somewhat
autonomous. It
does not know what it is, has

no desire to identify with anyone, has
no point of comparison, and does not
hold out for spring or for the radiator
to spurt, guzzle, and churn.
Snow is more like punctuation than a fragment
of flag such as "flake" suggests.
It is the dull and predictable repetition of the period,
or the pointed, bending arc of the comma.
It can pierce, too, an exclamation
and there can be "much snow"—
so much that it is remarked upon in a
"poem," which should also be a non-count noun,
a word of accumulation and drift.

Enter on the Left

"I feel you" is how she
announced her empathy, a capsule advertised
as containing the most potent form of protection
but also prevents fatigue
so the poem can remain on a pile of cobblestones,
left intact as a modest monument
to the avant-garde.
Now it's a memory: a massive crack
in new asphalt that makes
a chasm at the base of a hill, a steep descent
to the place where the road ends in a cemetery wall,
a perfectly terrifying T junction.
Autumn closed up like a cliché, both necessary
and empty, following failed
or perfect intentions everywhere.
At the funeral, we made small talk
with relatives. Our words
either failed or were completely perfect
or knew both failure and perfection at once.
All their mature poems were about time, too;
sooner or later, they would not have been offended
by a word or idea
that when heard at the wrong time
ricochets inside.

Strange but True

I know that sentiment makes an unflattering uniform
or that it should be better instrumentalized.
Given the resistance of the poem
to smiles and charm, its multiple correspondences
did not amount to a recovery
despite the persistence of dedicated staff
in the intensive care unit.
At the end of the day, we all know
nurses must wash their own uniforms.
We talk in the laundry room at strange hours,
between shifts.
This time
the memory arrives as perception
of difference, names
music as the way to know.

A Held Note

I overdramatize and underdress.
Silence permeates the space between them.
Perhaps conversation is overrated
but to save speech means also
to accrue its impossibility, if that can be measured.
I want to come to language without restraint,
without the general malaise of expenditure,
touch it by the softer light we use in the evening,
sleep with it, the space of two breaths between us.
Is it time to write or read? When the finished draft
seems an abomination of perfectionism,
an inflamed membrane,
I recoil
into silence,
listen to Arvo Pärt's *Alina*.
At the end of our life's narrative,
we will return to the volcanic island of our birth.
I will overdress for the occasion,
a movement resolved.
The avant-garde will
pour more silence
through its deep green shadows.

The Sculptor's House

What is in a mid-life year: a celebration of tameness
bookended by desperation?
I can hear it stirring: a disoriented
flock of gulls groans, scolds,
and mocks in chorus.
Every recollection has four unused niches
while *to use* is the most troubled verb.
This is not a toothache but it tingles
like the knowledge that a post office
will be just around the corner.
In fact, each step was hand-hewn
and beyond the balcony's cool stone
drifted three pink clouds.

Eva Hesse's Arrows

Arrows are directive. Without context, they point only at their directionality.

How does a simple grey-blue grid express such melancholy?

A faded leaf on the sidewalk in midsummer.

Smudging, too, is melancholic: it obscures a straight line, a structural limit.

It's all reduced to three straight lines that don't meet, an open triangle.

On crowded sidewalks, we move as a singularity.

Noon ushers in four straight lines.

The east wind becomes an arrow.

The image becomes an arrow.

You want to tell me, "Go here!" or "Go there!" or "Look at this!" so you use an arrow.

We stop answering our messages.

Without soft fabric, they are stripped to structural dimensions.

St. Augustine's Arrow

In the margins of a medieval text,
a doodle of St. Augustine
aiming an oversized arrow
at a false allegation.

Her wrist gripped
by a hand that also tries
to hold hard to her memories,
to own them, as though
she herself could be without,
less, even, than another sample of passive
chagrin or impression of private sadness.

Poetry still carries a quiver of moral arrows it does not use.
I write in a time that begins and ends with self-representation.
Therefore every arrow points only at itself.
Can poetry put down its quiver, which has become a burden?

This is where we obliterated the thread of memory
threatened by the shifting balance
and weight of power over desire.

I suppose they'll relinquish his responsibility
in another essentialist dispute.
It's a phrase
I did not choose
but perhaps it's necessary
to dispell ghosts
to let them echo
one more time.

Palm Reading, after Joan Mitchell's *No Rain*

it makes counting seem both necessary and absurd

she dropped a thread
in the hollow
burning space
behind two eyes
that together see only one flaw

when pressed, the flowers faded to mere lines

we concocted perfume in the recesses of time

disintegrating yellowed petals surrendered all form to

the waves

the facility of becoming green or blue in nature

the faculty of recognizing happiness deep within oneself

the shadows they cast are unremarkable and owned by no one

and these colours heighten their wired attachment to trembling

Island of Broken Arrows, Incandescent, Transient

Their most expensive properties
overlook the empty, open courtyard
of Central Park,
shrouded in feudal mist.

Sovereign hierarchies of vertically occupied space and soundscape.

Another example
to add to the list of Frank Lloyd Wright's
forms of "artificial rent":
        the tyrant's voice gains undeserved volume
        and interest, raising itself exponentially.

Moving Platform

this late September dogday
I walk to Chelsea with a valise and two ice
coffees one with milk one black
though I don't drink mine
and the cup blows off Lee Ann's rooftop table
only a tiny sip is left

I've arranged a bouquet of arrows
at the last moment it's only a journal
chaos to be alloyed with punctual adjectives
composite flowers be damned
across the bridge of lettrism
a margarita and some savouries
Unity Movers on 8th Avenue
pause to recall it is wicked it is weak
rotating their divine wheels
after a conversation about poetry
I'm blindsided by a rape trial in the senate
or lathe which is another sort of tongue
twisting its silenced *e* into memory
"his hand over my mouth"
to be voiceless then to testify
literally, figuratively

a labellum is the large central petal of an orchid flower

they explain how you can win
a bid at an antique auction
for liquid added to the position
of the living not dead   having no middle
position, supposed energy points
constantly shift location.

irrationally I will touch the bottom of the sea
with this one breath
this is one dose of naturalism
and then we'll take the bright blue stairs
leading to the sign of Libra
a pair of scales
a weight on each equivalent
to the given name of a lover

set free the phone receiver falls to
the table   resounds
and the voice continues
recalls something signals
personally
in simple intervals

Plot Line, after "The Green Years" (*Os Verdes Anos*)

Who moved from the country to the city.
Who possessed a sharp mind but no financial means.
Who lived in a spare room at their uncle's and felt like a burden on their family.
Who quickly became bitter.
Who was never able to reconcile her expectations with theirs.
Who learned to navigate bourgeois spaces of automatic doors and escalators, traffic and street lights.
Who started to smoke and drink and bite their nails and stay out all night wandering.
Who wondered why their lover carried on flirting with other lovers.
Who wondered whether they were narrow-minded and barbaric.
Who grew ugly in their thoughts when they should have blossomed.
Who desperately married and divorced a week later.
Who poisoned themself with cheap chords and cloud promises.
Who collected food stamps but was too proud to exchange them.
Who was whisked by taxi to safety to escape a stalker.
Whose belongings fit in one bag they could carry in a taxi.
Who had never purchased luggage, nor did it occur to them to do so.
Who could never afford to fill a piece of luggage with belongings.
Who dismissed shopping as a "brusque affair of binding meaning to the self."
Who soon stopped smoking and drinking and going to nightclubs.
Who was searching for an exclusive exterior that would return them to optimism.
Who resembled their parents more and more each day.
And then he stabbed her with a knife. I wasn't expecting it. I believed she had escaped.

Relocation

rhododendrons
great footway
on the other side broadly speaking of exploration
several fine hemlock a foot trail east side
running from in order to return
unusual still pond water
still the hemlock groves known
as Poison Pond
by anyone attempting
to return

while there are several fish
there is no certainty
it's seldom dry

at Poison Pond in order to return
after parking for a small fee
by the dirt road
and hemlock grove
along a tract in the foreground
a future tense measures the view
of disastrous conditions
overlooking
word slopes
and marked paths
across
Saxon Woods
paralleling

instead of
petty arguments about betrayal
or tearful
glacier ponds

she watches for him
at a refreshment stand
will follow the crest of the hill
to call him father

meeting with fog or cloud

and follow the equestrian path
of about three miles
the road goes under
the Putnam tracks
instead of passing under
the gap

and up Letterrock Mountain
to the shelter at an unmarked trail
crossing a path unchosen
for the southwest ridge by switchbacks

Colour Debts

Goya maintains a lively and loving correspondance with his schoolboy friend Martin Zapater until his death. They exchange letters but also parcels containing dresses, linens, sausages, and even dogs, back and forth between Madrid and Saragossa (a journey Goya's drunk courier Delgado can make in two days). As close as a brother, Martin pays for Goya's mother's upkeep after her husband's death. When Goya loses his hearing, the letters grow longer. He sends his friend furniture for his new home, including a canopy bed with painstakingly written instructions on how to set it up and operate the curtains, to be fastened by the foot of the bed with pins or ties. *If I was not indisposed, I would have arrived there this evening and set it up myself, and then spent the night. Wouldn't that have been nice!* But the century has another life in store for Goya. Losing six children, losing his hearing, then losing his professorship because of his disability, Goya sees his growing list of artistic achievements increase in proportions inverse to the devastation in his life. After he loses his hearing, he loses a large part of his income. He eventually secures funds to pay his colour grinder but is forced to abandon colour debts he owes to a pharmacist: light ochre, dark ochre, fine ground crimson, black earth.

Demolition

Goya buys a villa called the Quinta del Sordo (House of the Deaf Man) where, with the help of his son, he paints fourteen or fifteen black wall paintings on the theme of witchcraft and melancholy, including the famous image of Saturn brutally consuming his offspring. These paintings were transferred from the villa walls onto portable surfaces before the building itself was destroyed.

Genitalia

At fourteen, Goya is tutored by a painter who works for the Inquisition as a Reviewer of Dishonest Paintings and whose job it is to add a swirl of cloth or leaf to cover the exposed genitals in the paintings of the old masters. Later, Goya paints the first depiction of female pubic hair in *Las Majas* and the first scene of fellatio in the shadows of *The Madhouse* (*Casa de los locos*). Elsewhere, I read: the prudish act of adding a fig leaf to cover the genitals did not emerge until the next generation of painters. If so, why did Goya paint men without penises?

Requiem

flight interrupted by sobs

held against incalculable disaster

circumstantial wall will

crumble

       bullet-ridden

orange and yellow

nasturtians risen

again listen and bloom again

through
       another

chain-link

fence

as though paper

airplanes

to the height of circumstance

launched but they will not

fly

through the organ

shot through with

(horrors oppose)

all that has to do with a long folded

wing touches its irreparable name

by the course of things
arrives
at its destination

in the discourse of happiness

a
----
will die on this day

to violence

civil horrors truly

and returns singing nevertheless

fly through the open glass door

of its embrace

or through sonorous clarity

through a parting

of nations

where the cruellest glass doors

of our own

whole

seem to meet

irreparable

one name is a form of gratitude

an achievement of form

another name is its subject

held over most cities

aerial photography is invented for surveillance

names inscribed

street names

names inscribed

     in creases of paper

pressed between fingertips and

pencil lines smudged

tips of names collected in a quiver

then loosed in flight

under Bow Bridge

criss-crossed shadows

rippled glass their name's

manner of civil flight

produces thirst and

the original reads

flight: a contraction for

failure of light

"in times like these"

Saturn consumes his own offspring

as signature attached to a string

an accident of filial regret

scripted empathy: I hear you

after another empty phrase of shells

Quiver

Cloud cover, an altar cloth, an infinite trembling.

Rambling rose with a creamy white, musk-scented flower.

A sign hanging on a saloon door prohibits handguns on the premises.

I pass this on my way to the university, where I am doing research in the archives.

In Austin, in August, I notice no one else walks.

Such intensity of heat is untranslatable: even shadows move heavily in the humidity at noon.

A confessional exasperation: I remember. A statement of hard, shiny, fusible insistence.

A metal-framed mirror and a human figurine, a wooden horse with broken legs, hard words and weathered words, warm and worn, the future tense and its finely detailed designs we pull over ourselves at night for comfort.

Hardwick

When asked if she was sexually active, she replied, "No, I just lie on my back."
I found this note on a scrap of paper lodged between book pages

on a small lending shelf in our basement laundry room, *Melanie Klein*, by Julia Kristeva,
and brought it upstairs to the apartment, to add to my growing collection, books I intend

to read one day and that are as familiar as friends. In what context is any object neutral?
When is neutrality an excuse for passivity? Lying in wait, over the next few months

we found ourselves far from home, long-term visitors in Hardwick, Vermont, a name,
I learned, that has nothing to do with candles, endurance, or the heart, but only a colonial

tendency to replicate an English place name. *Hard* as in *herd*, *heorde*. The news from home
percolated the same burnt aroma daily. There was discussion of "herd immunity" beside

the horrors of losing loved ones, untraceable in the wick of quarantine, buried incorrectly.
A dichotomy of solitude and gathering made more sense in Hardwick than in the city.

At the end of the driveway stood two black bins for trash and recycling, for moving objects
outward and away. The road, a narrow grey strip, solid and unbordered by sidewalks,

communicated cloud cover in wait for the spring that did not happen. Ferns emerged whole from
the snow cover, no fiddleheads to speak of. Emily Dickinson's crocuses,

like closeted love notes, were buried in full bloom. It's a type of currency,
snow, in an economy of pain, and also contains *an element of blank*. Erasures

in the lifelong love story of Emily and Sue are still repeated, despite the evidence.
The refusal to see will go on longer than we were promised but we are not waiting. We laugh

watching romantic pastoral films, like *The Bridges of Madison County* or the BBC
documentary *The Good Life*, at this idea of countryside as escape, baring

onself to the unseeing wind. Now, is it more dangerous to identify as a lesbian
than as a potentially infected New Yorker when in a traditional, rural area, exposed

by one's marigold-yellow licence plates (the colour of leftover taxi paint)?
Daffodils finally bloomed close to my forty-fourth birthday, crowded together

like gorgeous people in a city park, worshipping sun. I want to document the settling dew,
the desires of windows, everything I see and everything I believe (not necessarily

the same thing). Precarity of labour, financial insecurity, social injustice: poetry, why
pretend these things do not keep us awake at night. I heard wind

gathering resistance through tremendous forests, rising and falling, tried
to distinguish it from the hard monotone of a distant engine, stagnant in volume,

inner sounds of the future, struggling for breath, and the secret *murmur of a bee.*
I feel the weight and warmth of our future as it collapses into me.

In the first minutes of 2020, I discover a dead bee at the bottom of my dessert
bowl, after raspberries consumed alongside a requisite glass of champagne.

Mummified, the dry, sacrificial bee stares silently. New York
is unusually tender when we wake later on January first, more itself

than usual. Marvellously ordinary while only neighbours come and go (but
just until noon). Next day, the champagne is not entirely flat. Velvet bubbles coat

the tongue in luxurious forgetting. *Because the bee may blameless hum
a bee for thee I do become.* I return to honey's inevitable meniscus.

Hardwick hiking trails are labyrinthine, shepherds' footpaths uphill alongside fields,
sugarbush trails through maples, poetry trail around a wooded creek. Water

moves on, without us. Throughout quarantine, I am as still
as a shelved object, as Emily's drowned bee. Galvanized

sap buckets hang from the wrong type of tree. Romantically, I pick up
his book, open it at random. Rilke writes, "The girl and the woman

will be but imitators of the masculine ways," in his *Letters to a Young Poet*.
I want to throw it in the creek. They will ask you what or who

is young. Who or what is girl or woman. What ways are masculine
and why should women bend to them. I'm done with literary history,

once again. This is a repetitive problem. First the poem was about Emily
Dickinson, then it was about Agnes Martin, then it was about Audre

Lorde, then it was about Gloria Anzaldua. There was no way
to bring this all together.

Briefing

how this is possible

how we returned

how I collapsed and my body folded into itself, an animal mound

how much I love you, as compared to then

for how many, the flag hung at half-mast

how I received the news and you

how with your eyes averted

how wounded that time

how I know

how incommensurate is suffering

I know: how impossible to compare

I know how long it has remained stable, not how long it will be sustained or whether

how, by a hair

how we knew only so much then and today we don't know enough to claim with any accuracy that we knew as much as we thought we did, and as to when we will know enough to make changes, that remains to be seen

I was quite still for a long time

In the hotel room, an image of a simple arrow is framed on the wall. It points nowhere in particular, nor is it much to look at, a representation of minimalist thinking in process. The room is a temporary residence. This is supposed to be liberating. The furniture is cheaply constructed, of contemporary design: a display of identical monochromatic straight lines that look orderly but are certain to warp in time. No matter, because no one inhabits the room for longer than a few days. The tongue of time passes over the teeth of the future with predictable swiftness as quickly as the wide band of light edging along a windowpane toward noon. The language of time can grant itself its own freedom.

The girl with the broken gaze is seated on the charcoal-grey sofa below the picture of an arrow, which points to the left of her, technically toward a television set that is never turned on. Rotund expressions flutter to the ground, on scraps of paper released from a notebook she pulls from her bag. She connects these scraps with more arrow drawings, with pencil and glue, collage work she does when no one else is home. She is distressed by the contemporary imperative to vision, which is why she is called the girl with the broken gaze.

If only the rain would rise up before it goes down. Symphonies of misery abound outside the painted walls of the hotel, in the neighbourhood beyond, where a funeral is taking place. We can no longer hear them. The noun swallows itself in poetry, where there can be an invisible rain before the rain of realism sets in. If time is clear, a noun consumes itself. This is not a matter of reduction but an opening outward onto the sea. The unanalyzed knowledge that waves just pretend to ignore us as they construct their patterns, the ocean is a wild beast, alternately thrashing and soothing.

The girl with the broken gaze collects arrow pictures. Arrows, she decides, are resolutely empty and therefore not words. But they may also be used as weapons.

In one frame, a figure plays music with a bow and arrow. She repurposes the weapon to repair a wound, or tries. In another, there are only wasted, broken arrows.

She sees the light and shadow of diurnal patterns and hears muted sounds of frolicking in the hallway. The imagination swallows itself and the memory of its temporal combination. A nearly steady ticking of old-fashioned clock hands, ticking arrows, in the distance, mimicking both music and weaponry.

Some words are a tremor in the lower eyelid of the girl with the broken gaze, or a tremor in the surface of water in a glass on a bedside table, when the ground trembles. In the meniscus, terrible reason prevails. The fault line of the earth is a leafless line, a faded crack in the reason for dreaming, organically crooked like a twig.

Words rain down through an open kitchen window. When this happens, she must guard herself against frozen words, which hurt if they land on the skin. A random silence needles her and provokes its own extension in time. It begins with when. When, it asks, does it begin? This pattern like leaves always predictably layering overhead, filtering all light, protecting one (yes, with a purpose, too) but never sheltering, so that the protection is flimsy, thinly translucent. Regret is like this. It is not a suitable dwelling. It keeps her dry in the present but only if there is no real storm or weather to manage. It would be better to live under an umbrella than under regret. It is without limits. It does not open and close like the sentence. Days in the hotel room opened and closed regularly, sometimes clustered into an event. That is memory. A series of events that are handed down. A string of event beads made of chaotic silence.

The chaotic silence is broken by motors, by helicopter shuddering, by six whistles of an alarm. It suggests the riotous as instantly as an arrow to rain down. To go back to when: it begins in such instability, in the clanging of memory's city streets. That's the first installment of panic. And then it is chaos again and silence again, split apart, open.

NOTES ON THE POEMS

"Direction of Flight"—The italicized line is from Alejandra Pizarnik: *"Como cuando se abre una flor y revela el corazón que no tiene"*

"Requiem"—"In times like these" refers to a line spoken by Charlotte Moorman, included in the exhibit I saw the day after Donald Trump was elected on November 9, 2016, at the Grey Art Gallery on Washington Square. In a video taken in the '60s, Moorman says, "In times like these you can't expect the kind of art you had before." "I Hear You" was a talking point that aides included in Trump's notes when he met with survivors of the Parkland school shooting. "Civil horrors truly" is from Thomas Carlyle.

"Hardwick"—Italicized lines or phrases are from *Emily Dickinson's Poems, As She Preserved Them*, edited by Cristanne Miller.

author photo: Jiyang Chen

Angela Carr is the author of three previous poetry collections, including *Here in There* (shortlisted for the A. M. Klein Prize for Poetry), *The Rose Concordance*, and *Ropewalk* (shortlisted for the McAuslan First Book Prize). Carr has also translated poetry books by Nicole Brossard (*Ardour*) and Chantal Neveu (*Coït*). She studied Creative Writing and Literature at Concordia University in Montreal, and later earned a PhD in Comparative Literature from the University of Montreal. She currently resides in New York City, where she teaches Literary Studies at the New School University.

COLOPHON

Manufactured as the first edition of
Without Ceremony
in the fall of 2020 by Book*hug Press

Copy edited by Stuart Ross
Type + design by Ingrid Paulson

bookhugpress.ca